SOME CHURCH

SOME CHURCH

DAVID ROMTVEDT

MILKWEED EDITIONS

Published 2005 by Milkweed Editions
Printed in Canada
Cover design by Percolator
Cover photo by Robert Meyer
Author photo by W. T. Pfefferle
Interior design by Percolator
The text of this book is set in Photina.
05 06 07 08 09   5 4 3 2 1
First Edition

Milkweed Editions, a nonprofit publisher, gratefully acknowledges support from Emilie and Henry Buchwald; Bush Foundation; Cargill Value Investment; Timothy and Tara Clark Family Charitable Fund; DeL Corazón Family Fund; Dougherty Family Foundation; Ecolab Foundation; Joe B. Foster Family Foundation; General Mills Foundation; Jerome Foundation; Kathleen Jones; Constance B. Kunin; D. K. Light; Chris and Ann Malecek; McKnight Foundation; a grant from the Minnesota State Arts Board, through an appropriation by the Minnesota State Legislature, a grant from the National Endowment for the Arts, and private funders; Sheila C. Morgan; Laura Jane Musser Fund; an award from the National Endowment for the Arts, which believes that a great nation deserves great art; Navarre Corporation; Kate and Stuart Nielsen; Outagamie Charitable Foundation; Qwest Foundation; Debbie Reynolds; St. Paul Travelers Foundation; Ellen and Sheldon Sturgis; Surdna Foundation; Target Foundation; Gertrude Sexton Thompson Charitable Trust (George R. A. Johnson, Trustee); James R. Thorpe Foundation; Toro Foundation; Weyerhaeuser Family Foundation; and Xcel Energy Foundation.

Library of Congress Cataloging-in-Publication Data

Romtvedt, David.
Some church / David Romtvedt.—1st ed.
    p. cm.
ISBN-13: 978-1-57131-422-2
(pbk. : acid-free paper)
ISBN-10: 1-57131-422-9
(pbk. : acid-free paper)
I. Title.
PS3568.O5655S66 2005
811'.54—dc22
                                    2005008403

This book is printed on acid-free paper.

For my daughter
Caitlin Belem

SOME CHURCH

ACKNOWLEDGMENTS

Thank you to the editors of the following periodicals in whose pages these poems, sometimes in different forms, first appeared:

BigCityLit (online): "Fixing Fence" and "Implacable America"
Borderlands: Texas Poetry Review: "The Bells of Balangiga"
The Cream City Review: "Gone"
The Drunken Boat (online): "Fixing Fence," "Still" (as "Not Rushing the Dance")
Georgetown Review: "Ex-Catholic Janitor"
New Works Review: "A Photograph of My Great-Aunt"
North American Review: "Door"
Pilgrimage: "Some Church"
Poetry East: "The Library"
Planet Jackson Hole: "El Segundo Ojo"
Ploughshares: "Once Strangers on a Train"
Prairie Schooner: "Buddha with a Cell Phone," "Homosexual Eyes," and "New Steps"
South Dakota Review: "Plums"
The Sun: "Rose"
University of Wyoming Alumni Magazine: "There's a Smell" and "Talking with the Governor After the Johnson County Fair and Rodeo Parade"
Voices: The Journal of the American Academy of Psychotherapists: "Rose"
Willow Springs: "Science"

"Talking with the Governor After the Johnson County Fair and Rodeo Parade" appeared in *The Poetry Pole Anthology,* edited by Jim Bodeen and published by Blue Begonia Press of Yakima, Washington.

"Plums" appeared in *Eat Our Words: The Montana Writers' Cookbook,* compiled by the Montana Center for the Humanities and published by Far Country Press of Helena, Montana.

Many people read and commented on these poems. I want to thank the University of Wyoming, and my students and colleagues at the University of Wyoming's Casper College Center who in many ways helped me write these poems: Bob Brown, Ryan Sandefer, Susan Thompson, Wendy Smith, John Kambutu, and Bruce Richardson. Thanks also to friends who read and commented

on the poems: Len Edgerly, Hugh Ogden, and Peter Sears. Mark Jenkins and
Alyson Hagy gave me the "Never Say Die" speech and kept me in fighting trim.
Floyd Skloot and Jane Sarmiento Schwab, aka Juana la Filipina, have faith-
fully, warmly, and critically supported my poetry for twenty-five years. Most
of all, I want to thank Margo Brown, who has read and commented on my
poems over many years and who has shown me that poetry is a part of life
but not life itself.

SOME CHURCH

SOME STARRY NIGHT

SPEAKING OF ANCIENT CHINA

By now the old Chinese poets are dead
and the world they knew is gone—
the night journeys in small boats,
the stars, the half-wild dogs,
the sound of the oars dipping into water,
the plum blossoms falling, or peach,
the moon like a plate of white jade floating across the lake
or like a perfect icy fruit impaled on a pine top.

The provincial governor writes note after note
summoning the poets to the palace and they don't come.
They're busy. Buzzed on cheap wine,
they stand up to shout poems at each other.
One of them falls out of the boat
and into the reeds where he is swallowed
by the moon's reflection and the wine bottle
goes into the water with both man and moon,
leaving behind the hidden huts on the hillside,
the scraps of food left on a plate behind the monastery kitchen,
the poverty including tuberculosis and pneumonia,
the everyday cold so that as the poets chant
they must now and again stop to cough or sneeze
or carefully spit phlegm into the black water.

I'm waiting for the return of those geezers
and the world they claimed as real
but they know I'm modern and impatient
and so they scramble out of the water faster
than I can see and throw themselves down
on their bellies in the bottom of the boat,
their eyes squeezed shut so tight
that tears leak from the corners,
their hands over their mouths to keep themselves
from giggling out loud. They're morons,

ancient though they may be, lifting their heads
to the edge of the boat so that I see the reflection
of the light in their eyes. "I'm gonna go home
and close my door," I shout. That scares them
and they jump up, making the boat rock.
"Ha!" I shout again and they shake their fists at me.

The thing is that poetry must not only help us feel good
but make us squirm. It's like those medieval princes
in Europe with their jesters and clowns who knew a little magic,
you know, coins from behind the ear, disappearing doves,
and who did gymnastics, a full flip over a table,
cartwheels across the great hall. And comedy, they knew comedy,
belching on cue, a headstand next to the roast,
the face of a dead pig and the face of a living man inches apart,
upside down to one another. Then out of the blue,
the clown tells the prince he's full of shit.
The prince frowns and thinks to have the fool's head removed
then applauds, remembering his duty to hear the truth,
to have his pride punctured.

Now pride is a virtue and the mighty do not seek to be deflated.
I wonder, are those Chinese poets still on their bellies in the boat?
Is that glittering the light from their eyes peeking over the edge?

BUDDHA WITH A CELL PHONE

The dark sky opens and it starts to rain. I go outside
to stand in the stream, the longed-for gift of water
where it hasn't rained for so long. I shout and dance
with the dog, who puts his ears back and licks my nose.
When we come back in, he shakes and I do too,
a few drops flying off my hair. I notice the Buddha
sitting on my desk. He's a rubber Buddha
in a yellow robe. If you squeeze him he squeaks.
He's got a radiant smile on his face, his eyebrows
happy half-moons over his eyes. As I stare at him
my wife walks by and with a cheery Buddha-like glint says,
"It's raining." In his right hand the Buddha's got a cappuccino
and in his left a cell phone pressed to his ear.
His lips are closed so I know he's listening, not talking.
One more thing—I pick up a little kaleidoscope
lying next to the Buddha and lift it to my eye to look outside.
I thought it would make the raindrops glitter
through the autumn-dry corn but instead what I see
looks like the ceiling of a great cathedral.
I whirl around and am presented with the image
of a thousand rubber Buddhas, each one
a drop of rain, falling, ready to hit the ground.

SOME STARRY NIGHT

The Greeks lay out in their fields. Who knows
what they were doing but in between
there was enough time to gaze upward
and drift longingly toward the stars
where mortal and immortal surely meet—
crowned heroes and garlanded goddesses,
a dog with its teeth bared and a monster
with more heads than ever it could lose.

It sounds lovely and it's no wonder
so many stargazing books are sold.
For what is life if not romance and longing,
hope and dream, deadly attractive delusion,
its magnetic needle hovering gently then swinging
deliriously from side to side as it comes into view?

The Greeks would not think like this—
no incentive for such thought
when the nights are warm
and one or two or three are busy in the fields.

I though have incentive, and time too. Time beyond measure.
My once and future stars shimmer down through the Wyoming sky.
I pull the book from inside my pack and take off one glove
to turn the pages. My daughter squeezes up next to me,
her left ski on top of my right. She too pulls off a glove,
clicks the flashlight on, and jams her hand back into the glove.
Golden clouds of breath float before our faces in the battery-driven light.

We click off the flashlight, shove the book back in the pack,
and set off for other cold climes. There is Greenland
and interior Alaska, and Saamiland far above Norway's snow.
We follow the creek as it rises and disappears into boulders,
track away from these, and keep climbing, the water gurgling

beneath rock and ice, the moraine reminding us of snows long past,
teaching us that even water can be made to move slowly
down the mountains toward the plains.

"More to the left," my daughter says. "There's the North Star."
Polaris, the one toward which the North Pole points,
but the pole moves and the earth wobbles
and the stars drift. Once Thuban in Draco
was our faint northern guide, and still to come are Deneb
and blue Vega, each brighter than Polaris but not yet ours.
I think that things seem to shine as they recede
and I wonder at the Greeks and at my daughter
skiing beside me, and at the unnamed stars
whose light bouncing off snow illuminates my way.
I stop for a rest and pull my water bottle from my pack.
I can't stop thinking of those Greek stargazers,
their bodies moist from the heat of the night,
goats browsing nearby, and wine and olives,
smoky torches making sloppy noisy light,
then a gust of wind and the torches grumble
and gutter out so that the stars hang in darkness,
knife points amid muffled expressions of wonder,
tiny cries of pleasure, ambiguous sighs.

My water's not quite frozen but when I drink,
the cold makes my teeth ache and my head pound.
"Boy," I say, "that's cold."
"Yeah," my daughter says, and on we go,
searching for the perfect spot where the snow is packed
and there's an opening in the trees.

STILL

The children are sleeping
and the cows and chickens are sleeping,
and the grass itself
is sleeping.
The machines are off
and the neighbor's lights,
a half mile away, are out,
and the moon is hanging
like a powdered face
in a darkened room,
and the snow
is shining under stars
the way we are shining here
in our cold skins
under warm quilts.
We pull our shirts over our heads
and toss them to the floor
and the only thing grotesque
is the space through which
we stumble each night.
I roll to you and put my hand
on your skin. You shiver and smile,
"Cold. But not too cold.
Some cold I like."
And draw my hand closer.
I pull it away
and jam it in my armpit,
and while I wait for the blood
I look at you, admire your face,
your neck and breasts,
your belly and thighs,
the shadowy double of you
thrown by candlelight to the wall—

There is no season, no grass
gone brown, no cold,
and no one to say we are anything
but beautiful, swimming together
across the wide channel of night.

IN SOUTHERN CHILE

The train slows and I lean
out the open window to breathe in
the salty air. Beso, the sign reads.
We are coming to a stop in a town
called Beso—Kiss, as if we might
fall to our knees and bend forward
to embrace the earth itself.
Or maybe we are meant to remember
those we have loved and kiss their feet,
rise along their bodies kissing
their legs, their bellies and arms,
the long dark hair that frames their faces
and that is blown by the wind from the sea.

"Beso," my wife says, leaning hard
against my shoulder, squeezing
into the narrow opening to look out.
"It's not on the map."
"No, it's a really small town."
"But the train has stopped here?"
"Yes, but I think for only a minute."
"¡*Beso!*" the conductor calls.
I can hear the click of his counter
as he passes, and feel him looking
left and right at the passengers, making sure
the number on board matches the number
of tickets he's taken.

"¡*Beso!*" he shouts again, then
"*Cuidado con la cabeza*"—Watch your head.
I pull back thinking he's speaking to me
then see he's helping an older couple
down the metal steps. He holds
the woman's arm and guides her.

When she is safely on the platform,
he returns and helps the man.
I lean back out the window,
my head again next to my wife's.
The whistle blows and there is a lurch
as the wheels turn, then turn again.
The old couple is walking to the waiting room
but now they turn and smile, wave.
I look around but can't see anyone
then realize they're waving at us.
We wave back. The man puts his arm
around the woman's waist
and nods. As we pick up speed
they walk slowly into the building.

"That's beautiful," my wife says.
"What?" "All of it—
the salt smell from the sea,
the ancient whistle of the train,
the train so close to the shore,
a town called Beso not marked
on the map, that old couple
wrapped in each others' arms."

She puts her hand on my head
and runs her fingers through my hair,
hard, leans toward me, so that if I turned
just slightly her lips would touch my cheek.

FIXING FENCE

Nobody I know loves fixing fence,
setting creosoted posts into ground
hard as rock, stretching barbed wire taut
to sing in rising wind and burning sun.
In the fall when hunters come
it's worse, wind-drifted snow, gates
left open and wire cut.
They would make for themselves
a straight line from kill to truck
and drag the carcasses across the ground.
Sometimes I miss these cuts and find
weeks later a band of sheep far from home.
Sometimes I find the cuts after a storm
when the trail is clear and it is cold.
Often enough it is a fence not solely
my own but one I share with a neighbor
and so I go and speak to him and we meet
on a day when the cold will freeze our feet
and hands. We wrestle with the wire
and the come-along and curse together,
saying "sonsabitches," then again,
grinning, "sonsabitches."
We find a fence post driven over
and splintered and I go to the truck
for another and we have to use a pick
and a bar in the frozen earth.
We put our backs into it
but it's no-go and we decide
to use magic—the levitation trick.
Instead of setting the post into the earth,
we let it float above ground,
held upright by wire pulled tight
on either side, rocks stacked around.
It works. "Sonsabitches!"

We drink coffee from a thermos.
In the cold I pull off my gloves
to set the fencing staples and drive them in,
to release the come-along and start again.
My hands are so dry the skin cracks
around my fingernails and I bleed.
This happens every winter.
I put bag balm on the split skin
and wrap it tight using cotton wads
from the top of the aspirin bottle
and a strip of greasy masking tape
I found in the jockey box of the truck.
Gloves back on I complain
but it is fine, the bright sun
and glittering snow, my neighbor
whom I like plenty well enough
and who does this work with me.
He is a smiling fat man—cattle
while I am sheep. When I say I'm sorry
about the cut fence, he looks up and says,
"Hell, don't bother me none. 'Sides, ain't
your doing, damn Eastern hunters."
I'm grateful he trusts me and believes
it is the hunters and not me cutting the fence
myself to let my stock onto his range
where they can get some free feed. "What
d'ya spoze them assholes is thinking anyway?"
"I don't know," I answer, "but I can bet
not a one of 'em ever fixed fence."
And I lean back and slam a staple
into a splintery post so cold
the creosote smell is gone.
Even in this cold I'm sweating
and I take off my hat to wipe my forehead,

feel the sweat freeze there. "Fences."
"Once upon a time," my neighbor says,
"there weren't no fences in this country.
My granddad can tell about it—
how there was herders everywhere,
every herder with his sheepwagon and dog,
some of 'em with a horse. You remember
that herder busted both his legs and somehow
drug hisself up on a rise then got his horse
to stand there on the low side and he slid
onto the horse and it walked on into town?
Resourceful son-of-a-gun." And he hits
the post again with a hard blow of the hammer.
"Fences. Always fixing 'em. Always
will be. Makes me think of how a big storm
comes and the wind drifts the snow
over the fence lines and sheep'll
walk right up and over into the next county
and on south. That's why I run cows
even if I know them old-time gods
don't want no fences anyways.
Knock 'em all down if they could."
Again, the hammer blow and the smile
and I look at my neighbor and realize
that he's a friend, hammer in hand,
staples in his mouth. We work through
the short near-solstice afternoon.
When the sun drops behind the rim
of the mountains, the cold comes on.
"Better go in," I say, and he says,
"I'll just get this and we'll be done."
So we work ten more minutes—
snowbank and shade, ice and light.
"Okay, then," he says, "looks good enough

for now. We can set that post
when the ground thaws."
"When the ground thaws?"
"Yeah." He laughs. "Next spring.
I'll see ya then."

GONE

Boom, goddam it, the bomb,
that invaded my sleep and waking,
the noise I can't describe,
my secret life, clicking and hissing,
the moments of deepest pleasure,
the sucking as air disappears from space.

I look down on my daughter's face as she sleeps.
She is more emissary than gift.
There is a union that each of us has with the other.
There is a real you reading this poem.

That was the bomb that rose
over the horizon line of my life—
the liver color, the mushroom cloud,
the river of fire, the invisible death to come,
the underworld bomb, the devil bomb,
the radioactive-cockroaches-take-over-the-kitchen bomb,
the planet-lifting-and-hung-upside-down bomb.

Now I live with the circus bomb, the carnival
sideshow bomb, the clown bomb, the cream pie
in his hand, the winds up and throws and when it hits
me in the face, or misses and hits my neighbor, the
ha-ha bomb, an explosion of laughter. By saying this,
I don't mean the bomb's less real.

It's just faith, or hope, an intuition
that things will be alright, that inside
the creamy filling there is a knife,
and though the blade is open and ready to cut,
it's not to kill us but to warn us, so we will wake.

MOLLY

I'm washing dishes in front of a painting of a strawberry.
Pins protrude where the tiny yellow seeds should be,
real pins, steel and sharp. A thud comes from the bathroom.
I wipe my hands on my pants and go to see.
Molly is sitting on the floor with blood pouring from her chin.
She is not crying though she looks surprised.
I set her on the toilet and ask what happened.
She was walking along the edge of the bathtub
and decided to fly. In midflight, she tumbled to earth.
Her chin struck the porcelain edge of the toilet bowl
and the skin opened through layers of flesh to bone.
Now a few tears come from her eyes but she is quiet.
I tilt her head back and look closely at the wound,
press a cold washcloth to the blood, draw it slowly away.
At the hospital, I hold her hand as the doctor stitches her chin
back together with needle and thread—seven large stitches.
Before the last stitch is drawn tight, I look into the cut
and there is Molly, in clouds, surrounded by sky.

HOMOSEXUAL EYES

In the hall at school where I teach
there's a poster encouraging the kids
not to drink. It shows a movie marquee
for *The Vivid Kiss*, PG-13. A young man
and woman embrace, the marquee lights
shine down on them. They lean into one
another and the woman looks up at the man
with a smile on her face. She is so fresh,
so young, so lovely. I've never seen such
happiness. The young man, too. The poster
caption reads, "This is a night to remember.
You're having a great time. Who needs
alcohol? You get to remember everything—
the way she looked, what he said—all the details."
I have to admit getting drunk looks pretty lame
next to this ecstasy. I read the words again—
what is to be remembered about a woman
is how she looked, and, about a man, what he said.
There's more—"Look around you. The night
looks pretty good on its own." It is the man
who does the looking while the night,
who is a woman, is looked upon.
But the young man is as beautiful
as the young woman and posters like this
are printed in the thousands and hung
on walls where people look at them and give
barely a thought—an exhortation not to drink,
a young man and woman about to kiss.

Imagine if that was all I could see.
Never two young men—a night to remember,
what he said, how he looked, the announcement
for the vivid kiss. Instead, a blank space,
an emptiness that hovers below the marquee,
the sparkle and shine from our absent homosexual eyes.

TWENTY-FIVE VULTURES

There are twenty-five vultures
roosting in my neighbor's cottonwood tree.
They rise in high lazy circles,
patient for what might be dead below.
The flap of their wings
makes a noise I hear from far away.

This is the third year they've come
to live here with my neighbor
and he never complained before.
But now, his wife dead,
and him shot full of chemo and radiation
for his own cancer, he's got a different attitude,
been calling the mayor's office and demanding
they do something. "Like I'm living in a goddam
chicken coop," he says, and asks me to help him.
"Mayor says it's the county—we'll go to the commissioners."
"But I haven't got any complaint about the birds," I say.
"Anyway, don't you have a shotgun?"
"I do. I do," he nods, "but them damned dirty birds
is protected. You shoot 'em and the federal boys'll be all over you."
I say, "There's nobody out here but us. No federal boys at all."

My neighbor calls up Game and Fish and complains.
A few days later a warden appears in a dark green pickup.
He aims a fat pistol up in the tree and fires.
There's a whir and a trail of smoke
then an explosion and whistle
loud enough to bust the walls of the house,
knock out the windows and scare the shit
out of every living creature in two miles.
The birds flapped off in a black cloud
and didn't come back for fifteen minutes.
The warden waited for them to settle down

then fired again. Each time the vultures
scattered, returning in fifteen minutes.
The warden shot four times then the sun went down.
You could see the silhouettes in the branches.
Next afternoon the warden came back
and did it all over. Bang. Scream. The dogs howled
and the cats took off for the lambing sheds,
the vultures flapped away and the sun went down.
I hoped my neighbor felt better for the attention he was getting.
After the second visit from the warden, the vultures were gone
for two days. When they came back, the neighbor called
again and the warden came again and bang, scream,
the pistol and by then I was rooting for the vultures.

Then it was Saturday and Sunday and Game and Fish
doesn't work weekends. I saw the warden in town
and said, "Those vultures are still there. They're tenacious."
The warden shook his head and smiled, "Once vultures pick
a roosting tree, they stay. Noise won't scare them away."
"Doesn't seem very useful then."
"No, not very useful." He touched the brim of his hat,
nodded, and left. I left too, thinking about my neighbor
and how would I feel if it was me who had maybe six months,
maybe two months, maybe only a few weeks left to live?
Would I go after the vultures?
I like to think I'd be too busy getting ready
to give myself back to the earth
so that if you were going to find me,
you'd have to look down like the vultures
and fly patiently in an ever-widening circle.
But I don't know. I might act like my neighbor,
call Game and Fish, fire the gun to make the explosion,
raise my face, shake my fist, and shout
I ain't dead yet, goddam it, so get outta my trees.

ONCE STRANGERS ON A TRAIN

When the poles clatter past,
the years fall away, a spider drops
from the petals of a flower, space
is ever more empty the larger it grows,
the steel wheels chunk-chunk-chunk
on the joints of the rails, the friction
making sparks, stars crushed
and invisible to us inside.

There is a distance that diminishes
as the point of departure recedes.
I fall asleep and my head drops
onto your shoulder. You let me
rest there so that when I awake
I can smell your foreign skin and feel
the wet spot on your blouse, my mouth open.

I hold you in my arms again,
harder than I did that first time,
harder than the glass holding us
inside the compartment, our bodies
inside our skin. I am only and forever
that man and you, that woman.

I whispered some word
and you held your hand up, shushed me.
We could hear a traveler turn in the dark,
uncomfortable, a slight groan or sigh,
all of us third-class passengers, our souls
sleeping on hard benches.

When you drop your hand to my lap,
I realize our lips are so close.
I feel your breath, then touch.

Where are we?
Where are the swallows
who bank and turn as we enter the tunnel?
The dust that rises as we pass?
The lips? And again, the kiss.

IMPLACABLE AMERICA

FUCK YOU, PATRIOTISM

I have apologies to make.
First, for the obscenity in the title
of this poem. I utter words
in heat, then feel embarrassed.
I try to withhold such hot
feelings but sometimes they
come out, like pimples,
no matter how old I get.
Or like my political opinions
that are at odds with those
of my neighbor, a man
whose car bears bumper stickers
reading, "Annoy a liberal,"
"Gun control means being able
to hit your target," and "Charlton
Heston is my president."
At least my neighbor knows
who his president is. I wish
I didn't have a president.

My second apology—
the more serious one,
the one I can't quite make—
is for writing a poem
whose subject is the nature
of being in the state, that is,
the politics of citizenship.
All my life, I have been told
that the political poem is a betrayal
of both poetry and person.
As a poet I should be whispering
to you of the breeze on your wrist
and leaning close to take your hand,
turning it palm up, brushing

my lips across your skin,
blowing gently enough for you to know.
But the gentle wind becomes a gale
and though I would hold you
with all my might, something
beyond us intrudes.

The Chilean poet Pablo Neruda
maintained that it would be difficult
for predominantly rational people
to be poets and just as difficult
for poets to be rational.
Still, it is reason, Neruda claimed,
that holds the upper hand,
and reason that is the mainstay
of justice and so must govern
the world. But I am unconvinced
that reason has shown its ability
to rule and, moreover, what
does it mean to say
"predominantly rational?"
Neruda himself wrote poems
of both politics and love and
was elected to the Chilean senate.

I understand why they told me
political poems are oxymoronic.
I too hate them and, like many
Americans, have read plenty
of polemics disguised as poetry.
I've sometimes felt disgusted by poems
about racism and oppression,
about military spending and war,
about hunger and AIDS and poverty

and the strange irony that my country,
the richest in the world, I'm told,
though my income provides only
tangential evidence of that wealth,
anyway, the strange irony
that my country has no
national health insurance.

I long for a poetry
of husbands and wives, parents
and children, lovers, flowers,
sowing and reaping, contentment,
even middle-class contentment.
There is enough pain
to fuel a rocket to the stars
and it takes no poetry
to help it on its way.
A poem that makes
a single human being happy
for a single moment is worth
all the rational words ever uttered,
all the protests,
all the bills passed in congress,
all the debates,
all the national anthems and pledges
of allegiances and Ten Commandments
posted in public buildings,
all the governing
and the welling up of patriotic tears
on behalf of the nation we love.
In this view—God Bless America—
patriotism is so much din and clatter.
Damn—that's a milder word than fuck.
And happiness—that's the poem,
no matter how badly made.

IMPLACABLE AMERICA

I lean back and fall into the crackle of cottonwood leaves
and dried grasses—the gold, brown, and gray. November day
and the sun roars across the sky, burning a last hole
in the clouds before winter arrives. On the other side
of the fence, pickups slide by, engine sound disappearing
into the distance of town, echoes and explosions,
America close and coming closer, implacable America.
Here and there along the ground are junipers, needles
a faded green, blue berries, hard perfume of the woods,
mountain mahogany bristling with spines. I throw a few
leaves into the air and the wind, as it riffles my hair,
carries these leaves away. Sun behind a cloud, it's chilly.
There's a tangle of sound from the creek, a low hiss
stumbling over exposed rock and bits of early ice that shine
in shadowy darkness. When I close my eyes, the water
surrounds me. The current doubles back on itself, carving
away the earth until the creek forms an oxbow and this land
is cut off from the rest. In winter, the deer cross the ice,
going back and forth until spring thaw, when they are caught
on the island. They step into the water to swim home
but some, as they bend down, see the wavering reflections
of themselves and halt, momentarily confused.

BUSINESS AS USUAL

I'm waiting for the phone to ring.
It's not a cell phone but advanced
technology all the same. When I answer,
I'll be on a conference call, business
as usual. No one suggests avoiding
the agenda, and instead addressing
whichever upcoming war is upcoming.
It's like death, which we'd rather avoid
but can't. In business, though, we
could avoid these discussions
but have them anyway. Perhaps
that's like death, too. I say this
thinking of my government's war
in Iraq, a war to show once and for all
who's boss. All wars are meant
to show whatever it is they show
once and for all. I look out
the window. Two days ago
it was ten below and snowing.
Yesterday it was fifty-five and sunny.
Now it's back to ten below.
I'm lucky my call hasn't come through
so I have time to write this antiwar poem
on my computer and so use another advanced
technology similar to the technology
my government uses to improvise death—
the invisible soccer players, unidentified
stock clerks, forgotten grandfathers,
boys and girls returning from school,
inconsequential and irrelevant individuals,
the flakes of snow that are falling
to the frozen ground. Some flakes
land on the wires that fill the sky—
household electricity, telephone, cable TV.

There's no wind so the flakes pile up
like nervous tightrope walkers, bodies
covered with goose bumps, teeth
chattering. Some are more confident,
though. They smile and wave from above.
A few even lie down on the wire and sleep,
rocking as if in a snug berth on a ship at sea.
When they fall, the snowflakes float
gently to the ground, as if pleased.
The phone rings and the noise startles
me. I jerk in my chair and bang my elbow
on the corner of the desk. I don't know why
it's called the funny bone. On the wires
nothing moves. It may be there is a balance
in nature, but the same cannot be said
of human life. There's the phone ringing
again. I grab the receiver and shout hello,
hoping that nothing bad will happen.

THE BELLS OF BALANGIGA

Balangiga, the Philippines, Sept 28 or 29, 1901

I.

They rang the bells and jumped
from hiding to attack the Americans.
Thirty-four men dressed as women—
heads covered, layers of extra clothes.
They carried small coffins. Why so many
women with coffins? "Please show me,"
a U.S. soldier ordered, and the woman,
opening the lid, displayed her dead child.
"Cholera," she said. The soldier
let the woman pass, the other women too.
Inside their robes were bolos,
heavy machetes the Filipinos used
to cut cane, to clear brush. A week before,
two drunk American soldiers went into a shop
to buy tuba wine and while waiting
tried to rape the shopkeeper. She screamed
and her brothers beat up the drunks.
U.S. troops rounded up 143 men—
every male over ten years old.
They confiscated bolos and destroyed
the town's store of rice. In response,
the thirty-four men as wailing women.
One of them, Capitan Valeriano Abanador,
grabbed Private Adolph Gamlin's rifle
and clubbed him. Then five hundred undisguised men
rose from hiding and killed American soldiers.
The American general asked, "How many
of our men died?" Maybe forty-eight or fifty-nine
or seventy-one. No one was sure. "I want to know,"
the general said and ordered the region pacified,
telling his troops to take no prisoners.
He said that the more Filipinos killed, the better,
the more houses burned, the better.

And tens of thousands died.
How many, no one is sure.
In these circumstances, my mother asked,
"Would you take up weapons?"

2.

When the Americans recaptured Balangiga
they took three bells. Two went to Wyoming,
to Warren Air Force Base. For a century,
the Filipinos have asked for the bells back
and the bells ring in the desert air, ring
through the smell of sage, a ship sinking
and the headlong rush to the lifeboats.
In the church above the post office the bells ring
for souls lost, souls found, souls forgotten.
There are remembered bells on winter mornings
and the girl across the street who in summer
rode her new bike around my house, ringing the bell
on her handlebar, skittering by, laughing and yelling,
"Look at my bike." And there's the bell choir,
the perfect white gloves of the players,
the Lutheran hymns, and the Jewish bakery
in Toronto where I went for my mother to buy bread.
I was in love with the baker's daughter,
nicknamed Bells. I never said it aloud
but I'd heard her father call her, "Bells."
My father told me to stay away from Jews
but I paid no mind and imagined I might say,
"A loaf of rye, please, Bells." She would turn,
surprised to hear me say her secret name,
and her father with his gray hair and sweet roll
in hand would smile seeing that I loved her.
He'd waggle his finger as if to say, "Go on,
go on," not blaming me so much for the past
through which I have lived but could not love.

LEGITIMATE OCCUPANT

When I answer the knock at the door,
there's a man from the Housing Authority.
"May I come in?" he asks.
Before I can answer, he's closed
the door behind himself and is looking around.
"I'm surprised to find you here.
How did you get this furniture inside?
And these books? May I see your ID?"

I think to refuse but then think
things will go better if I cooperate.
When he looks at my papers,
he seems startled but I pretend
I don't notice.

"Look," he says, "I can help you
move out. I'm not supposed to do this
but I live pretty close.
The legitimate occupant's moving in
at the beginning of the week."

The legitimate occupant?
It's my apartment.

He looks embarrassed and pushes
some papers at me, a lease.
"I've got a lease," I say.
He jerks slightly. "Look
at the name on it. That guy's
got the same name you've got.
And look at the picture. Go ahead.
That guy could be your twin brother."

Of course he could be my twin brother.
It's my name and my picture,
my apartment.

The man has gone into the kitchen.
"You wouldn't think to find two people
like that. The same, I mean.
It's weird. What are these plants in here?
They need watering." He opens
the refrigerator, lifts a dirty coffee cup
from the counter and sets it in the sink.
"You ought to clean this up. I could
help you. You got any boxes?
I could help with that, too. I'm not
supposed to, you know, but I live
pretty close. Just don't tell anybody.
Man, you got a lot of stuff.
Like you been here for years."

He takes the lease back and shakes his head.
"If I didn't know better, I'd swear that was you.
You ready?" He turns his head like he heard
a knock at the door. "Uh-oh, better get a move on.
We can come back later for this stuff.
You can stay with me."

He takes my arm and walks me to the door.
When he opens it he looks both ways
down the hall then pulls me outside.
In the hall I see the man from the photo.
He does look like me. But he limps.

"That guy limps," I say. "He can't be me.
It's my apartment. All you have to do is look
at the furniture, the plants, the books, the food
in the refrigerator. Who else would have that stuff?"

"Shhh," the man says, "I think he's seen us.
Let's hope he doesn't notice.
Come on, I don't live too far from here."

THERE'S A SMELL

Cutbanks and ridges,
and, in winter, cornices
that threaten to tumble and fall.

The whole rutted, jagged land
running from me to Powder River
and there's a smell of sage fills it all.

Takes me back to my childhood home—
dry country far from Wyoming.
Eastern Oregon dust which fills my mouth.

Tempts me more than any perfume
could tempt a man toward a woman,
the smell that covers other smells,

those we call our own and wish to bury—
armpit, early morning stale breath,
feet trapped too long in socks and boots.

All of this is sweet and attractive to me,
draws me to men and women, old and young,
animals rank and perfect in their way.

Every smell I can name,
I seek it, wondering what are we that we seek
some distillation that will make smell invisible,

the sage I told you,
the strange sulphurous fumes where the oil wells pump,
the dryness of pine closing in on the creek where there is water.

The hint of molds, mildew recalling wet places near the sea,
or by mountains where rain fell ninety-eight days in a row.
Stopped for a day and started again.

I go to town and there are the young girls, heavy with distance,
the young boys not far behind, their parents and the gentlemen
who rule the small towns in which we live,

the schoolteachers, blind and overconfident
telling us how to live—how to read and write,
to be American, to succeed, and all without thinking why.

What smell do they carry—fear and denial.
But even that, as it leaks from their pores,
I love and want to embrace them,

kiss their eyelids and arms
and call to them that we enter this world
rupturing and spilling our smells.

The world's smell,
this most living of forces.
Give up trying to sweep it away.

Step closer,
lean in, breathe, inspiration and exhalation,
respiration, secretion, excretion, all belonging to all.

EL SEGUNDO OJO

Yoselin, age four, has received her new eye.
Born with only one, it's important to have an artificial eye
in the empty socket. Otherwise, the face grows unbalanced.

My older daughter Rosalie has been tear-gassed
at a peace rally in Colorado Springs. Along with many of us,
she hoped to encourage the American government
to abandon its plan to invade Iraq.

Tear gas. The burning. The tears.

"Two eyes," Yoselin says. "Tengo dos ojos."

"Sí, claro," I say. *Orgulloso.*

She is proud of her new eye.

The old eye is still under there.

Today I took part in the Virtual Peace Rally—
impossible to get tear-gassed—
people from all over the United States called
their senators, even the president.

"What is going on with our dictator?" a friend
asks me. But I am more reasonable than that.
I say, "Hello, I'm calling to voice my opposition
to the war in Iraq. May I tell you my reasons?"
I get through to the offices of my senators,
and their aides sound sympathetic. But the White House
line is impenetrable. Busy busy busy.
Finally, the phone rings and I prepare to speak
but it's only an electronic voice that says,
"All circuits are busy. Please try your call later."

Like ten years from now.

"*¡Mira!*" Yoselin shouts.
She's smiling and blinking, showing me
there are two eyes in her head.

Here I am, dialing again,
trying to talk to people I can't see,
and the president,
not seeing people to whom he talks.

Then there's Yoselin, at four,
with her new artificial eye,
who sees pretty well.
And Rosalie, at twenty-four,
blinded by tear gas,
who sees best of all.

WINTER ROOTS

Long winter and the parsley waits with the rhubarb and iris,
the dog who lies on his back by the fire, his legs splayed out
and rising above him like roots upside down plunged into the sky.
Suspended from clouds in dream. Time to rest.

But those who would shape the world in their image do not rest—
the generals and governors, the presidents and prime ministers,
the surgeons and priests, the schoolteachers planning their next test,
the policemen bent over pulling weeds, those unconscious resisters.

Some green soul comes up wondering if it might be spring,
buds nipped by an ice storm, snow piling up on the spinach and kale.
Kale, a word that sounds like kill or keel or coal, the earth guarding
its fire, waiting, as stone and water, as you and I, dormant and pale.

CONCERT

Bob Dylan in Casper, Wyoming, unheard
of, so I drove down, blowin' in the wind
and the times they are a changing, me
and a bunch of fifty-something-year-olds
remembering when we were young
and so was Dylan and maybe something
really might change. Now it seems
there never will be any change. Christ,
I meet teenagers talking about stock portfolios.
Whatever's driving them, it's driving us all.
New cars, summer homes, theater-quality
DVD players, computer-controlled toaster ovens,
snorkeling holidays in Belize.

Dylan walked on stage and if it wasn't a swagger,
it was a walk of confidence. He stood upright
and he turned and called to his sides and smiled,
a slight man but not frail, not weak, electric and sure.
Blue eyes. He faced the room and we were one,
in the past. Then the sound, somehow sweet,
like he sang for God, but beyond good or bad.
It was some song we all knew and around me
people were singing along and I was amazed
to silence, listening to the music swell in the air
and even the air said welcome to whatever filled it.
Every mouth was opening and spilling forth
its satisfaction—kisses, procreation, transformation—
the perfect balance of the man on the high wire.

Suddenly, it was over. There was scuffling and cursing
and we herded ourselves into the night,
into the black asphalt parking lot, the rows and rows
of steel and glass, the rubber tires and the whirring sound.
Someone honked and someone else slapped a hand down

on a sheet-metal hood or trunk cover. "Shut the fuck up!"
I heard shouted, and then "I love you too." Look how many
people came to this concert in pickups. I wondered if there is
any other place where Dylan could give a concert and half
the people would arrive in pickups. I laughed and somebody said,
"What's up, buddy?" "Oh, nothing, I guess I'm just kinda
talking to myself." "Talking to yourself—that's not so good
for you. Come on over and sit for a minute. Talk with me.
Gonna take a while to get outta here, so many people."
I sat down next to the man on the tailgate of his pickup.
He offered me a beer from a cooler in the bed. "Thanks,"
I said. I took a long swallow and shivered, the cold beer
bubbling down my throat, the cold night. I was satisfied—
better, I was happy. I watched the drivers jockeying
for position in the parking lot, gunning it here and braking there,
and now and again, in the distance, I heard someone scream.

TALKING WITH THE GOVERNOR AFTER THE
JOHNSON COUNTY FAIR AND RODEO PARADE

I've been appointed poet laureate of my state.
Granted, it's the least populated state in the union
and one which many Americans can't place on a map.
Still, I could receive no greater honor.
But I offer few thanks and seem, I'm afraid,
not quite present. The fact is, I've been babysitting
a friend's dog while she's away in Denver
getting some culture. Someone has opened
the gate of my yard during the parade and the dog,
a longhaired dachshund named Abby
whose ears fly like wings when she runs,
has disappeared. I imagine the screaming
and the sounds of gunshots—even though blanks—
the roar of motorcycles and diesel generators,
and the whining of the go-carts driven by middle-aged men
in red fezzes, have combined to terrify the dog.

She's gone and my friend is going to kill me,
poet laureate be damned. So I don't properly
thank the governor, and disappear into the crowds
asking people if they've seen the lost dog.

A few hours later, a policeman comes by to tell me
he saw a little dog lying in the middle of the parade route
on her back as if sunbathing before the horses
arrived to crush her. He picked her up and put her in his house
and now he's brought her to me to see if she's the one.
"Yes!" I shout in joy. But it's too late
to thank the governor, who is already gone.

Well, poetry—they say that poetry is more often than not
against the ideals of normal social life.

And so the governor takes a risk—
not in naming me poet laureate, but in
naming anyone to such a post. The risk
isn't for what a person might do or say
but for poetry, what it is and might be.

COMING INTO THE FAMILY

COMING INTO THE FAMILY

My mother screamed in what she told me
was the agony of childbirth. I've tried
not to feel that I was the cause of her pain
though it's hard, since it was my birth.
She'd known for quite some time
that I was facing the wrong way
and hoped that I would turn. But I didn't.
One doctor wanted it to be a normal birth.
He put his hand inside and gently explored
until he found me and forced me around
so my head was pointed in the right direction.
Still, I didn't move. By now there were two
doctors and the second used forceps,
trying to pull me along. My mother
tried to help, pushing hard. "Don't push now,"
the doctor said, "I'll do it." But the forceps
didn't work and my mother couldn't stop screaming.
My heart rate dropped. The first doctor,
the one who wanted a normal birth
and who was young and slight,
my mother remembered,
put his hand inside again, this time
somewhat frantically and clumsily.
The cord was wrapped around my neck.
The young doctor cried out.
"No time," my mother thinks he said.
They cut her open and lifted me,
her first child, into the world.
I had bruises on my temples,
and one ear was twisted and torn
but I was alright. They sewed my mother up
and she was alright, too. Still, each of us cried
and was worn and there remain scars,
clear enough for us to see.

INFLATABLE COMPANION

I don't know what led to it—something we said or did.
My mother was furious and grabbed my brother and me
by the hand. "Okay," she said, "okay then, let's go."
We got a cab downtown. The lights were shining
and the store windows rattled. There was a woman
leaning on the wall. She was wearing high-heeled shoes
and I remember my brother leaned over and whispered
"Dad calls those fuck-me pumps," when he thought
our mother wouldn't hear. But this woman's shirt
was transparent. "You can see her boobs,"
I whispered back to my brother. "I heard that,"
my mother said. "Don't say boobs, it's vulgar."
She slapped me on the side of the head so my ears rang.
When I looked up again, I thought the lightbulb
above the woman's head had exploded.
Bits of glass came tumbling down like electric snow.
"Don't repeat things," our mother said to my brother.
She stopped at a door with a sign that read "XXX."
"What's this?" my brother asked. "What does that do?"
"Where do you put those?" The clerk watched us
but said nothing. Neither did I. I wasn't about to say boob,
that was for sure. There was a row of naked women,
like giant Barbie dolls. Our mother dragged us around,
grabbed our faces and breathed on us, hot breath.
"You like this, huh, you like this?" I started to cry
and she slapped me again, this time on the face
so my nose stung. Then back to my brother,
"Keep your eyes open, Little Man." She picked one,
said to the clerk, "We'll blow it up here. You got a pump?"
"No, ma'am," the clerk said. "Doesn't matter. Blow,"
she said to us. "You'll have to blow hard to make her big.
Right there, that's where you blow." She paid the clerk
and when the doll began to approximate a human being,
she took us outside with it. "Okay, let's go home boys."

She started walking. "We gonna get a cab again, Ma?"
She shook her head no. It was twenty-seven blocks
and a lot of people watched us carry that inflated rubber
naked woman home. Our mother started dinner
and told us to play. We dropped the doll on the floor,
uncertain what to do, where to look. On the bottom
of the right foot was a label that said "Mimi."
She lay still as a dead lady. Her inflated boobs
stood up straight like little mountains or scoops
of ice cream or baseballs or I don't know.
Her eyes were open like a real dead person,
like my great-grandmother who when she died
I was just a little kid but I went to the morgue to see.
I started to cry again. It was just my father and my brother.
Our mother didn't want to go. When our father said to her,
"It's your own grandmother," she answered, "I know."
They wheeled Great-Grandma out like for another operation.
When they lifted the sheet, I saw her boobs
lying off to the sides of her chest, falling down
like they were as dead as she was. I knew
she would have been embarrassed but I kept looking.
My dad said she was his wife's grandmother.
When we went outside and the sunlight hit my head,
my hair felt crackly like it was full of glass
or full of sand like when we went to the beach
and played all day. It was always hot and the sun
was always shining. Before we went in the house,
my great-grandma would brush the sand off my arms
and out of my hair and the grains would swirl around me,
tiny pieces of light tumbling out of the sky.

THE LIBRARY

My grandmother didn't read much
and she never wrote but I go to the library
to be with her. It's always warm there,
too warm like her house as she got older.
She'd wear a sweater on a summer day.
In winter, she'd crank up the thermostat.
"It's so hot, Grandma," I'd say, and she'd answer,
"Not to me." January afternoon, the slate light fading
to gray, thirty-six below, I walk wrapped as much in memory
as in my coat. Until the last four days of her life,
she'd never been in a hospital except to visit friends.
Before she died, she sat up and looked out the window
at the cottonwood leaves she'd seen for ninety years.
She said a few words, nothing too deep, a little story
of once upon a time. Her mouth smiled while her eyes
frowned, intimating that she knew something but wasn't telling.
Then she squeezed my hand, and was dead.
Because I'm a writer, they asked me to speak
at her funeral. It was cold like now and the ground
had been hacked open for the grave. The county snowplow
was parked north of us as a windbreak. It was like being
next to an elephant for the first time, that shock at how big it is.
And a snowplow is yellow—unremorsefully bright
against the mourners' dark clothes, the brown frozen earth,
the gray sky. I actually did prepare a talk but when I stood up
between the snowplow and the hole in the ground,
all I could say was, "She had a life." I felt bad
but no one seemed to mind. Afterwards, we scraped the ice
off the cars' windshields and drove back to the church
where there were tables of food in the basement.
I couldn't eat and walked away to the library.
The thermostat on the heater had broken and
it wasn't just warm, but hot.
I started to take off my coat
then stopped, sat down, and left it on.

DAILY WALK

My grandfather steps out from his furnished room,
looks left and right. Here are the luscious lawns,
emerald green under the water being sprayed
through the oncoming dusk, the long light
at day's end making the droplets gleam.
Also the weeds and fields of dust, the rows of cars
at Marty "No Bull" Eggers Chrysler/Dodge/Jeep,
the man smoking in front of the Second Chance Store,
the former driveways leading to vacant lots,
houses that are no longer there though the trees
planted years ago now lean far out into the street,
cottonwood and ash and weeping birch, the leaves
that come and go as if the seasons were signs
reading "Then," "Now." Grandfather checks the street.
"I can still walk," he says, his own steps
between the past and the present. He stops
to touch a branch or to take a juniper berry
and crush it between his palms to make a paste.
Among bricks and vinyl, aluminum, asphalt, and glass,
the faraway smell of green in dry hills, little noises
in the wind, the manmade rubbing up against the not—
these grasses and flowers, bushes and trees, the last
survivors of other days, or pioneers of days to come,
days of rain, days of sun. "I have plenty of hope,"
my grandfather told me, "even though I'm old."
Finally my grandfather steps out of his body,
leaving his skin on the sidewalk where a passerby
might kick it into the bushes, where it might be eaten
by grasshoppers, or curled by drought.
When we have bodies it is easy to defend them.
We arm them with bombs they lob at other bodies.
I look at my grandfather's face—steadfast and still.
I hope there is a bomb that will land on human motives
or at least on corporations and cars. In school we studied

the tea ceremony of Japan, the tea masters who knew
"what heart's ease there is in a gentle deformity."
Even at seventeen it made me stir—what heart's ease
there is in a gentle deformity. Another skin
left behind, an idea, or a word, a human being
as lovely as a plant, doesn't matter, left behind.

A PHOTOGRAPH OF MY GREAT-AUNT

It's 1938 and she's a young woman.

"You never talk about your family,"
I say. She doesn't answer.
"You look so young," I try.

"A person doesn't stay young forever,"
she says, implying something.

I hold my breath thinking she might go on.
When she married she refused to convert.
I'd like her to explain—the family
is Catholic, Lutheran, and Jewish.
So which temple is ours?

She coughs, says, "It's the only photo I have
from before the war. Everything else was lost."

"Yes?"

She's sitting by a window.
It's dark outside and the sky is heavy
as if it might rain. I turn on the light
then realize too late it's a mistake.

She waves her hand as if the past
were too worthless to bring back now.

I ask no more questions
even though I feel that I'll explode
from wanting to know.
No more questions,
but I can't say if my silence
is out of respect
or only fear.

MY GREAT-UNCLE'S LAST JOB

It surprised him that men and women
would come in together. They'd look around
without looking at him, walk along the rows
of books, videos, peep rooms, appliances.
Even when it was crowded, it'd be real quiet.
"It was a job," he told me, "available
because people will buy and sell
just about anything. When I landed
from Norway, I worked unloading boxcars
of rough-cut lumber in Bridal Veil.
There were trees everywhere and wood
was being shipped in. It wasn't the weight
that was hard as much as the splinters
through your gloves. Every night I sat
cutting them out with the blade of a knife.
I'd miss a few and they'd fester until the bubble
of skin broke, releasing the pus. After the boxcars,
I set chokers in the woods, rain and fog and cold.
I lost a finger when I set a line, signaled okay,
and two links on the chain twisted and pulled up
short. That was it for the woods. In Quilcene,
I bluffed my way onto a framing crew.
That was better than the cables, the snags
twisted every which way, chainsaws, and mud.
Nothing's perfect, though. With framing,
there are roofs to fall off of, and the same rain.
A man sets a nail then gives it a blow home
and, as the nail goes in, the water gushes out.
People worked anyway. If it's never dry,
you work wet. I had two daughters
and did right by them and their mother—
paid the bills and never hit them like my dad hit me.
I'm proud I could help both my girls go to college.
Finally I fell off a roof. 'Landed on your head wrong,'

the nurse said when I woke up. I told her, 'Hell,
there's no way to land on your head right.'
After that it was the wheelchair.
I still had to have a job. It's funny—
they've got a ramp—a handicapped-accessible
porn shop. I laugh but I'm embarrassed.
I can't even tell the grandkids what I do so I talk
about the old days—the boxcars and the woods
and how I lost my finger. They love to feel
the stub space. I'm teaching my grandson
how to use a saw and a drill and a chalk line.
I'm going to teach the girl too. Why not?
After work, I go to my daughter's for dinner.
Sometimes I help the kids with their baths.
I run the water, get their clothes off
and get them into the tub. I wash their hair
and try not to get soap in their eyes.
I slide out of the chair and sit on the floor
by the tub. That's how I do it.
I want to tell the kids about their grandmother,
how when two people love one another,
a part of them becomes one,
a part of them becomes like God.
I'm a differently abled clerk
in a porn store talking about God.
Doesn't even seem odd.
I pay my own way.
Sometimes I pick up a magazine
and look, and I have to check the videos
when they come back. Maybe a customer
forgets to rewind the tape or worse,
the tape's screwed up—picture flipping
around or covered with black-and-white snow.
If the picture's out for more than a few seconds,

we get rid of that copy. The owner
lets me keep half of anything we make
selling defective stock. First time,
I said, 'Five bucks and you can have this one.
It's good except for that one spot.' The customer
blinked, said okay, and nodded, reaching for his wallet
so fast I knew I should have asked for ten."

ARRESTED

I was a working-class kid from southern Arizona
who wanted to go to college. Not just any college
but one I thought was good and important
so I would be, too. It had to be unusual, radical.
Not Harvard or Yale, those holding tanks
for America's business elite, for those anointed by money
and historical privilege. I picked this place in Oregon
called Reed, applied, was admitted but didn't tell
my father because he would say I couldn't.
He thought college was a waste of time.
He thought I should get a job as a musician.
That would keep me from busting my butt laboring like he did.
He said that playing music would be a good easy way
to make a living. On the day before I left home
I told him about college. He said, "No. You can't go."
I said, "Yes, I can." And drove three days to Portland.
My father called the Arizona state police
and reported me as a runaway so the Oregon state police
had to pay a visit to Reed. No one wanted to arrest
a boy for going to college and between them all—
the dean and the policemen from two states—
they convinced my father to let me stay.
When I tell people that college was the most powerful thing
that happened to me, that it changed my life,
I feel good and I hope that other young people
can have such an experience. But now my father is dead
and it occurs to me, after so long, and you'd think a smart boy
like me could have figured this out way quicker, that my father
knew this and feared that my change meant I would be lost forever
to the world that gave me birth, his world. And so, with no other tools
that would do the job, he gave up and tried to have me arrested.

DOOR

I'm alone now but I forget
and come thumping up to the back door,
loud in my work boots, louder
when I bang the mud and shit off on the wall.
It's best not to surprise my father.
I pull my feet out of the boots and rattle
the door, stick my head in, and shout, "Hello!"

No one answers and I remember he's dead.
Feeling first relief then shame then both,
I go to the kitchen and run water from the tap,
gulp it down, wipe my mouth on my sleeve,
wipe my hand on my pants. The house is still.

I hear him talking—you know, in my head.
I can't make out the words but the tone is tender
and so I wonder. I step down the short hall
to the bedroom he shared with my mother,
the room of shouting. I put my hand
on this doorknob and stop breathing.
He's singing, "Grab your coat and get your hat,
leave your worries on the doorstep . . ."
I laugh and the breath bursts from me.

When I step into the room,
the light swims in with me
and falls onto the chair like a body.
My father's leaning over the bed,
now wordlessly humming the tune,
unfolding clothes and laying each item out—
a blue dress, a pale yellow blouse,
several pairs of women's underwear,
shoes, hats, and gloves. He runs his hands
over the material, buttons and unbuttons a coat.

Without looking up, he quits humming
and starts to talk again. "What?" I ask.
When he looks at me, I'm not there.
I've always recognized my mistakes
only moments after I commit them.

While I believe the universe is infinite
I don't think the dead can come back.
Still, here he is, finishing the last buttons
and tossing the neatly folded clothes to the floor
where they lie, a jumbled mass. He steps forward
and pushes me against the wall, lifts my arms
above my head and pulls my shirt off
then tosses it on the heap with the rest.

This is the only thing I have over him now—
my naked body. Or is it the stuff—
the shirts and shoes and buttons,
the dishes to wash and the fields to till,
the infrequent dinner parties
and the hat that keeps off the rain?

When he lets go of me and stumbles away,
my arms float upward as if undaunted by gravity.
He smiles and lets his arms rise too,
but only for a moment. Turning back
he points at the heap on the floor.
I'm tempted to ask "What?" again
but I think I've learned my lesson
and anyway he's no longer talking
and I don't know if he means to give
the clothes to me or to take them away.

THE WORDS

I was born in the fall,
in a house I can't remember.

At three I rode in a car,
the night-dark trees rimmed in silver,
the moonlight bathing the road.
My father pulled over and turned off the headlights.
The stars fell and clattered against the roof, the trunk, the hood.

At fourteen I wanted to escape.
I learned easily how to talk.
It was harder to be still.
The planets rotated as they rushed through space
while the moon drifted rigidly, refusing
to turn, one side light, the other dark.

At twenty-seven I slept along the shore
of a great African lake.
In the rain I threw potatoes
into the embers of a steaming fire.
I pulled them out and ate,
leaning back on my haunches
under a blue plastic tarp,
listening to the monkeys chatter
in the green canopy above,
watching the clouds through the trees.
I lay on the wet ground
and shook with the fever of malaria.

At thirty-four I watched bombs fall toward me
and, along with many others, fled.
At night we sat in darkened buildings, curtains
across the windows. The gunfire was distant
then close then distant again. When we felt safe,

we turned on the television and huddled around
to watch *telenovelas* from Mexico City—
the pale blondes whose dresses grew tighter
as their deceit grew deeper,
the matriarchs protecting their incompetent sons,
the businessmen fathers measuring their fortunes, and so on.

At thirty-eight I saw my daughter born.
The tomb came forward and fell back.
Animals approached the house
and pressed their faces to the glass.
The baby cried then slept.

At forty I was filled by a religion
that had no creed or dogma—not even a name.

At fifty I found that I had awakened a poet,
a man both close to and distant from
the story I call "my life."
See how things are speeding up,
I said to myself. The words
turned, as if they'd heard me,
and left the room. I followed them
out the window and across the rooftop.
At the roof's edge they leapt across
and I, thinking what the hell, did too.
That first time I landed fine,
but I could stumble and if I do,
if I turn an ankle or break a wrist,
or worse, I like to believe
that I will get to my feet
and keep on running.

NEW STEPS

I only had so much wood
and so many nails
and no money to buy more
so when I built the steps
I made four instead of five
with a rise of eleven inches.
I convinced myself it was okay
but my grandmother took one look
and said, "How do you think
an old person is going to climb those?
You ought to tear them out,
and build new ones." "These
are the new ones," I said,
but I found some old dowels
and added a railing. She said
it did as much good as a television
to a drowning man. It gnawed at me
so I borrowed the money and bought wood—
ropey utility grade—scavenged an old sign
from the women's shelter, cut it up
and used it for fascia. The new steps
had a rise of five inches. "That's good,"
Grandma said, "I can climb those.
But look at them, all raw like that,
if a person were barefoot, she'd
get splinters. You should sand
and paint them." I wanted to say
they were fine but stopped,
realizing I'd never seen
my grandmother barefoot
though I knew barefoot
is how a young girl
would run up the steps.

SOME CHURCH

PLUMS

Here in Wyoming it is possible to grow plums, but barely.
My trees stand twisted and short, the wind heaving at them
and the snow piling up in drifts along the south wall
where in summer the heat might let blossoms turn to fruit.

I planted a final tree beside the deck
so that when I sit the light comes dappled down
through the leaves and litters the pages of my book,
pools of light and dark through which I go on reading.

Once in twenty years we've had plums, small and hard
then slowly growing larger, the matte dusting of blue
almost like the sky. It's not so much that I wanted
to eat the plums, but to have them meant something more.

And so I went on reading and thinking about what purpose
any of us has beyond the moment in which we sit or stand,
roll our shoulders and shake our hair, hop on one leg
just to know we can and then laugh or shout at a crow.

The afternoon went on and the light came longer, beams
drawn out, somehow hotter than earlier in the day. I turned
and reached toward the tree, pulled a plum off and ate it,
and the flesh was warm and yellow and not too firm.

HEART

The men learned that a single woman
had moved to town. "I hear she's still pretty,"
one said, and another asked, "Pretty what?"

The first went up there with his hat in his hand.
She came to the door in a battery-powered cart,
joystick steering, big tires, and a bumper sticker
that said, "I don't brake." "Excuse me, ma'am,"
the man said, "I think I got the wrong house."

That was the end of the courting but she gets out
in the cart, goes everywhere. I see her on the road
and we talk. At Christmas she called and asked me
to come into town. She'd baked cookies, wanted
to give me some. "Thank you. I'll come right in."

When she handed me the cookies, I said,
"They look like my grandma's doilies." She laughed.
"They're Scandinavian, made like shortbread."
"Well, you'd think I'd know, me being Norwegian."
Smell like my grandma's perfume, I was thinking.
She wrapped them up in aluminum foil for me.
At home, I sat in my chair and tried to eat one
but it was too sweet. I hated those cookies
but I loved her for making them and set
the aluminum foil package beside the toaster
until February when I threw the dried crumbs
out on the snow for the birds to eat.

That spring she told me her son had been killed
in a car wreck. That's why she moved.
They took his heart out and put it into the chest
of an Armenian soccer player. "That guy would have died
but my son died instead. After he got out of the hospital,

he visited me. He was sitting on the couch
then he knelt down and bowed his head.
He reached into his back pocket for his wallet.
I thought he was going to try to give me money
but he pulled out a drawing he'd made of Jesus.
He told me Jesus brought him my son's heart.
He held out the drawing and started to cry.
He was so happy I couldn't ask why Jesus
would take my son's heart and give it to him.
He offered the drawing to me but I told him
to keep it and so he put it back in his wallet.
The angel that was my son, smashed in the dark."

ROSE

My second child, unexpected after so many years,
is born and I am mysteriously amazed at how
Rose, her older sister, seems suddenly grown up.
Here she comes now, eight years old, her hair
cropped short on top and left silky long in the back.
She's wearing a red short-sleeve blouse and a necklace
of obscenely large red beads, like blood fruit of some kind.
She's squinting into the sunlight and her jaw is clamped shut.
It's hard and juts out, though not in an unfriendly way.
The baby has set Rose to thinking and she asks questions.
She and I have a facts-of-life dialogue and the next day
she goes to her mother and says, "That's disgusting."
Her mother says, "Rose, someday your body
is going to tell you it wants to be with a man like that."
It wouldn't have occurred to me to say that.
Rose's eyes swell up like moons and her mouth
hangs open like a black hole. "No way," she says.
"No sir, not me. When my body tells me that, I'm not listening."
The other thing is that Rose has become fascinated
by religious thinking. She asks me to read the Bible to her.
When we get to the part about the Virgin Birth,
she says, "Oh, that's nice, read that again."

SOME CHURCH

I'm sitting alone on the extreme right side
of the Cathedral in Mexico City, down close
to the altar and the people passing, stopping
for a moment, genuflecting, lighting candles,
dropping large coins in the metal can. The calm
is not, for me, so much a spur to prayer as an opening
to emptiness, to the grace of being nowhere.
The Cathedral is leaning to one side. Ironically,
it's the side that abuts the Templo Mayor.
Some city workers were digging to find a leak
in the sewer system and discovered an Aztec holy place.
Now more and more of that holiness is being uncovered.
The Spaniards built their church on top of the Templo Mayor.
They did this throughout Mexico, thinking to bury forever
any trace of the people they were to become. Now,
five centuries later, the blood of the living and of the dead,
of the Spaniard and of the Indian, all mixed up, and the Cathedral
is sinking into the earth, the Templo Mayor rising back into sight.
In the Zócalo, men wearing sunglasses and Aztec costumes
dance in the heat, black and green feathers around their heads.
Their legs and arms shine from sweat, brass ornaments jangling.
The Cathedral, obscured by scaffolding, is being lifted and leveled.
Motors roar, pumps and generators, complicated layers of pipe
and board. Men stand in the air repairing cracked walls,
the shiver of matter. Inside, there is the same scaffolding,
along with halogen work lights on tripods. Brilliant pools of light
flood the dark walls. And again, workers are leveling and plastering.
Among the pilgrims, there is one who has stopped.
He's craning his neck to look up, apparently as interested
in the mix of stone and lime as in God. The sea of people
parts to flow around him. He takes off his hat and wipes his brow.
He's wearing brown shorts and I'm surprised they let him in
with his uncovered legs. His cheeks are a florid red
and the skin is flaccid on his neck and upper arms.

His loose shirt is soaked in sweat. He fans himself
with the English-language brochure from the Templo Mayor.
I look up as he did and find myself whispering, "Some church."
As if I were a man able to stand comfortably in awe.

FIRE BY THE LAKE

It was the dry season and the hills burned.
In the night, the fires flowed up the slopes
like rivers of gold flowing against gravity.
Some things refused to panic—the plants
consumed by the flames, the exposed soil
that grew hotter, the rocks that began to shift
and roll, the night itself, remaining black.
Good, I thought, we're still following the laws
of the physical universe. I waded into the water,
pleased to find that I shared the darkness
with domestic and wild animals—dogs and deer,
foxes and goats. We'll build a boat, I said,
let me run get some wood. With no urging,
they turned and swam to the center of the lake
where it was too deep for me to stand.
I thought we were sharing this, I shouted.
I lifted my hands above my head
then brought them down so that the water,
smoking in sympathy with the flames, splashed up.
When it fell, it was as rain. Glorious, I said,
and went on slapping the lake, the animals
in the distance, swimming hard, not looking back.

FIRST COMMUNION CERTIFICATE

Here is the official responsible for the doors
to the church. "First communion certificate?"
he asks. "Lost in a fire," I say. We live forever—
forget the certificate, forget guarding the doors.
He holds up his hand. "Look out!" I say, grabbing him
and making us spin around. Put that way, it's confusing.
"Look out!" could mean there's something wrong,
or it could be a hurried request drawing one's attention
to the world—the cottonwood tree along the ditch,
the stones I turn over in my garden each spring.
I think I saw that stone last year but maybe
it's a new one. I get out my magnifying glass
and toss the stone from palm to palm, wondering
why the skin on my hand is named for a tropical tree.
I squat on my heels and jam my fingers into the dirt.
In a few weeks seedlings rise—spinach, lettuce, radishes,
and beans. A tiny piece of mica clings to a leaf.
I flake away bits of the glassy mineral to make
a window, then hold it up. Look out again!
Here comes the official back up the steps to the doors.
He grabs the mica and says, "It's the sky but it's blurred
because mica's not as clear as glass." "Stained glass?"
I ask, then see it's my first communion certificate,
the one I thought I'd lost.

CONFESSION

Sometimes God is an open sky, blue upon blue,
sometimes closed, gray clouds building
toward rain. Then God is the rain
that may or may not fall.
When I drink a glass of water,
I swallow God and when I urinate,
God splashes onto the ground.
I breathe, inhaling a million Gods
and exhaling a million and one.
That one flaps her tiny wings
struggling to keep up.

Sometimes God tumbles
out of the sky and I step on him.
He cries out in a language I recognize
so that I think he is some baby bird
fallen from its nest.

Sometimes as I walk
I am dreaming of a better life
and then I am trying
to make this better life real.
I step on bird after bird
until my shoes are slick with blood
and I slip and fall.

SCIENCE

The country's full of flies. I hang a bag of pesticide
from a tree so that the cows can walk back and forth and rub.

There is a glacier in the mountains above town,
fall and tumble, but every year the ice recedes.

Some laugh to see slugs copulate, hanging by threads from trees.
Others say this is not so much funny as perverse.

The honeybee's enemies nestle in her hair. Hungry,
they tickle her mouth. She feeds them sweet nectar.

Angels, pictured as both male and female, engage in neither
photosynthesis nor heterotrophic acts, and reproduce asexually.

There is a star so magnetic that at the distance of the moon
its attractive power would rearrange the molecules in our bodies.

Archaeologists believe that certain delicate phials
found in Roman ruins were meant to hold tears.

LONGING

Before bed, I step out of the house and hear longing.
Sometimes I think it might be coming from distant stars,
but mostly I know I'm a psychic radio telescope.
I send out a signal, and that signal comes back to me.
I hear my thoughts from outside my head—things I wish
I'd done and places I wish I'd gone. I go inside
and there's my wife waiting for me in bed. I feel
the appeal of her unannounced still-secret powers
and of her smooth skin, the curves of her breasts.

But I feel other powers calling. Not that I'm hinting.
I know change can be just another word for disaster
and I don't want to make too much of my longing,
which is ordinary and which I own no more than I own
the earth on which I walk, or the child to whom I am father.

"Are you alright?" my wife asks, and what touches me
is her sincerity. I mumble some claptrap
that even I can't understand.

That night I dream an old enemy has become my admirer,
and tells me I'm brilliant, a genius. I say, "I know, I know,"
and smile so that my words will be taken as a joke.
I'm hiding the fact that I think I *am* a genius,
but when I wake, I feel ashamed.

In the morning we eat under a cottonwood tree.
The wind comes up and leaves tumble down
into our hair and onto our plates. I love this
and leap up, running in circles like a dog,
trying to get up the nerve to bark.

EX-CATHOLIC JANITOR

I was the guardian of the church—the floors, the walls,
the double doors, the coyote and the palm painted on the arch.

Every Easter we use colored sawdust and make designs in the streets.
The procession passes and destroys what we've made.

Some men threatened the priest. They waved pistols at his head.
I showed them my cell phone and they fled, but I was shaking.

The animals come inside for the blessing of the pets—cats, dogs,
lizards, frogs, a lot to clean up after. Once, I found a dead parakeet in a cage.

It's an old church built by Indians under the direction of Jesuits.
Now tourists come and drop film canisters in the flowers.

Here is where people begin the yearly pilgrimage to Magdalena, Sonora.
They bow down and ask for favors from the bones of Father Kino.

"By God" is a good way to begin almost any sentence
and it works whether or not you're a Christian.

NOTES

Page 6 "Some Starry Night" takes as its source Richard Kenney's poem "The Starry Night," which appears in his book *Orrery*.

Page 8 "Still" follows "Danse Russe" by William Carlos Williams.

Page 10 "In Southern Chile" and "Once Strangers on a Train" (page 21) were inspired by Pablo Neruda's *Cien sonetos de amor*. The first follows directly from Sonnet II, while the second tries to take something from the general feel of Neruda.

Page 12 "Fixing Fence" is a response to Robert Frost's "Mending Wall." My earliest memory of Frost is seeing him read at the inauguration of President John Kennedy. Frost had to be helped to the podium. The wind was blowing the pages of the poem every which way and Frost's hair kept falling into his face. Between the two, Frost could hardly read what he'd written.

The inaugural poem was about the land being ours before we were the land's. Frost said that she was our land more than a hundred years before we were her people. I don't know if Frost meant to be patriotic. I go back and forth on the poem, in one moment thinking that it reflects willed ignorance while in the next moment thinking it shows a hope that one day Americans will be shaped by their land and quit trying to shape it.

Page 16 In writing the poem "Gone," I thought I meant that a certain fear was gone but I'm not so sure. My first book of poems, *Moon*, included a note to the reader stating that when the book was published in 1984, the people of the world faced daily the possibility of annihilation in a nuclear holocaust. In the note, I stated my hope that by the time a reader found the book the threat of nuclear war would be long gone and my words would seem a little ridiculous, that it would be hard to imagine a world in which nuclear weapons had once been a part of everyday life. I also noted that if there were still nuclear weapons, then we must all continue working to banish such weapons from the world. Well, we still have nuclear weapons and the world seems, if possible, an even more quixotically cruel and unstable one than it did in 1984. In 2005, citizens in the United States lived as if in a fortress under a government that behaved as if the rest of the planet was a mine or factory serving the ruling elites in the U.S. Life in 2005 was one in which the people of the earth faced widespread hunger, nearly perpetual war, declining standards of living, increasing corporate intrusion in every aspect of life, and astronomical disparities in the material resources accorded to the rich and the poor. On the other hand, we're still here and for that I remain an optimist.

Page 31 "The Bells of Balangiga" On September 28 or 29, 1901 (both dates are cited in historical texts), Filipinos launched a surprise attack on U.S. soldiers stationed in the town of Balangiga on the island of Samar. At least 48 troops of Company C were killed. General Jacob H. Smith, put in charge of pacification, began a brutal campaign of retaliation. Major Littletown Waller testified that General Smith instructed him to kill and burn and said that the more Waller killed and burned the better pleased he would be, that it was no time to take prisoners, and that Waller was to make Samar a howling wilderness. When Major Waller asked Smith to define the age limit for killing, the general replied, "Everything over ten." The secretary of Batangas province estimated that during the war 100,000 of the province's 300,000 people were killed by combat, famine, or disease.

Page 33 "Legitimate Occupant" follows Agha Shahid Ali's "Vacating an Apartment" from his book *The Half-Inch Himalayas*.

Page 36 "There's a Smell," "Concert" (page 41), and "Heart" (page 66) derive from my reading of Walt Whitman's "Song of Myself" that appears in his book *Leaves of Grass*. I've never understood the apparent contradiction between Whitman's sense of the goodness and inevitability of American Manifest Destiny and his clear commitment to the rights of all peoples. For more on this, see June Jordan's essay, "For the Sake of a People's Poetry: Walt Whitman and the Rest of Us" in her book *Passion*.

Page 38 *El segundo ojo* means "the second eye." The other Spanish in the poem translates as follows:
Tengo dos ojos—I have two eyes; *sí, claro*—yes, of course; *orgulloso*—proud; and *Mira*—Look at this/that.

Page 40 The poet Diane LeBlanc wrote to me from Minnesota sending a poem she'd written based on a greeting card reproduction of a painting by Cara Scissoria. The painting showed four women who were, from the shoulders down, turnips. Their hair was the filamentous end roots of trees. The women seemed to be hiding their eyes or awakening from a long sleep. The painting, the card, LeBlanc's poem, and now my poem are all called "Winter Roots."

Page 51 In "Daily Walk," the mention of "what heart's ease there is in a gentle deformity" comes from *The Unknown Craftsman: A Japanese Insight into Beauty* by Soetsu Yanagi.

Page 60 "The Words" is my version of Nazim Hikmet's "Autobiography," which appears in his book *Things I Didn't Know I Loved*.

Page 65 "Plums" was inspired by William Carlos Williams's "This Is Just to Say" and by William Stafford's "Thinking About Being Called Simple by a Critic."

Page 68 When "Rose" was published in *The Sun*, the last two lines read: "When we get to the part about the Immaculate Conception,/she says, 'Oh, that's nice, read that again.'" I received several letters noting that I had confused two Catholic articles of faith. The doctrine of the Immaculate Conception states that the Virgin Mary, in order to be pure enough to become the mother of Christ, was conceived free from original sin. Her soul was created in the purest holiness and innocence. Still, she came to earth as a result of the sexual union of her parents. The doctrine that pleased Rose was that of the Virgin Birth. This derives from the miracle that Christ was conceived by the Holy Spirit and born of the Virgin Mary. Mary had asked the angel Gabriel how she, who was a virgin, could become the mother of the Messiah. Gabriel told her this would be by the power of God. That's what pleased Rose. I'm grateful to the readers who corrected my mistake.

Page 71 When I began writing "Fire by the Lake," I was trying to tell about my experience in Jalapa, Nicaragua, where in 1988 I helped to build a children's park and playground. It was near the end of the Contra war. The Contras made up the American-funded military force that during the decade of the 1980s engaged in a bloody war to overthrow Nicaragua's Sandinista government. One day while I was mixing cement for an outdoor basketball court, American jets flew from Honduras to bomb northern Nicaragua. In denying the presence of the American jets over Nicaragua, U.S. President Ronald Reagan implicitly denied my existence. Other things I'd planned to include in the poem were a hammer and nails, worms and birds, dogs and cats. As I wrote, the poem refused to remain what I had intended. Nicaragua became confused with Guatemala where the fire occurred. In Guatemala, people build fences out of chichicaste, a kind of stinging nettle that burns like hell. There were no fires after the bombing run in Nicaragua and when the real fire occurred, there were no deer wading out into the water with me. The lake was huge though and I did end up out there watching the hills burn. I can't verify the death toll in the kingdoms of the plants and animals but in every war these are among the victims. All this is central to how the poem was made. For a more cogent comment on the issue, see Frank O'Hara's poem "Why I Am Not a Painter."

Page 76 "Ex-Catholic Janitor" was influenced by the Mexican poet Carmen Boullosa, whose work can be found in *Reversible Moments: Contemporary Mexican Poetry*.

ABOUT THE AUTHOR

David Romtvedt was raised in southern Arizona. He is a graduate of Reed College and the Iowa Writers' Workshop, and was a graduate fellow in Folklore and Ethnomusicology at the University of Texas at Austin. He has worked as a carpenter, tree planter, truck driver, bookstore clerk, assembly line operative, letter carrier, blueberry picker, ranch hand, and college professor. With the Fireants, he performs dance music of the Americas that is influenced by the music of Louisiana, Texas, and northern coastal Colombia.

Romtvedt is the author of *Windmill: Essays from Four Mile Ranch*, two books of fiction—*Crossing Wyoming* and *Free and Compulsory for All*—and several books of poetry, including *Certainty, How Many Horses, Moon*, and the National Poetry Series selection *A Flower Whose Name I Do Not Know*. A recipient of the Pushcart Prize, an NEA poetry fellowship, an NEA International Program fellowship, and the Wyoming Governor's Arts Award, Romtvedt currently serves as the poet laureate for the state of Wyoming.

MILKWEED EDITIONS

Founded in 1979, Milkweed Editions is the largest independent, nonprofit literary publisher in the United States. Milkweed publishes with the intention of making a humane impact on society, in the belief that good writing can transform the human heart and spirit. Within this mission, Milkweed publishes in five areas: fiction, nonfiction, poetry, children's literature for middle-grade readers, and the World As Home—books about our relationship with the natural world.

JOIN US

Milkweed depends on the generosity of foundations and individuals like you, in addition to the sales of its books. In an increasingly consolidated and bottom-line-driven publishing world, your support allows us to select and publish books on the basis of their literary quality and the depth of their message. Please visit our Web site (www.milkweed.org) or contact us at (800) 520-6455 to learn more about our donor program.

Turning Over the Earth
Ralph Black

Urban Nature:
Poems about Wildlife in the City
Edited by Laure-Anne Bosselaar

Night Out:
Poems about Hotels, Motels, Restaurants, and Bars
Edited by Kurt Brown and Laure-Anne Bosselaar

Astonishing World:
The Selected Poems of Ángel González 1956–1986
Translated from the Spanish by Steven Ford Brown and Gutierrez Revuelta

This Sporting Life:
Poems about Sports and Games
Edited by Emilie Buchwald and Ruth Roston

Morning Earth:
Field Notes in Poetry
John Caddy

The Phoenix Gone, The Terrace Empty
Marilyn Chin

Twin Sons of Different Mirrors
Jack Driscoll and Bill Meissner

Invisible Horses
Patricia Goedicke

The Art of Writing:
Lu Chi's Wen Fu
Translated from the Chinese by Sam Hamill

Boxelder Bug Variations
Bill Holm

Playing the Black Piano
Bill Holm

The Dead Get By with Everything
Bill Holm

Butterfly Effect
Harry Humes

Good Heart
Deborah Keenan

Furia
Orlando Ricardo Menes

The Freedom of History
Jim Moore

The Porcelain Apes of Moses Mendelssohn
Jean Nordhaus

Firekeeper:
Selected Poems
Pattiann Rogers

Song of the World Becoming:
New and Collected Poems 1981–2001
Pattiann Rogers

For My Father, Falling Asleep at Saint Mary's Hospital
Dennis Sampson

Atlas
Katrina Vandenberg

Interior design by Percolator.
Typeset in Photina by Percolator.
Printed on acid-free 50# Glatfelter
by Friesens Corporation.